This book belongs to

_____

This book is dedicated to my children - Mikey, Kobe, and Jojo.
When you own your breath, nobody can steal your calm.

Calm Ninja

By Mary Nhin

Pictures by
Jelena Stupar

Calm Ninja earned the nickname, Coolio, because he was as cool as a cucumber.

And that's because no matter the circumstance, Calm Ninja could stay very calm.

For example...

When Calm Ninja found out his brother ate his candy without asking, he would simply say...

When learning how to play a new instrument, he remarked...

And if he was getting yelled at, he would answer...

All right mom, I'll try it like that next time.

Calm Ninja was very calm but there was a time he really could get quite impatient.

While doing schoolwork, he would get anxious and say...

The Calm Ninja Yoga Flow

I can stand tall like a mountain.

I can bend like a cat.

When I exhale, I can moo like a cow.

Here's my downward dog.

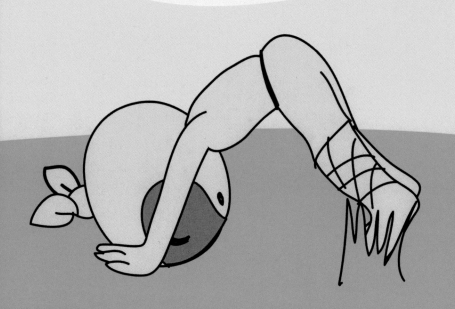

I can slither like a cobra.

I am brave like a warrior.

I am strong like a boat.

I am as powerful as a lion.

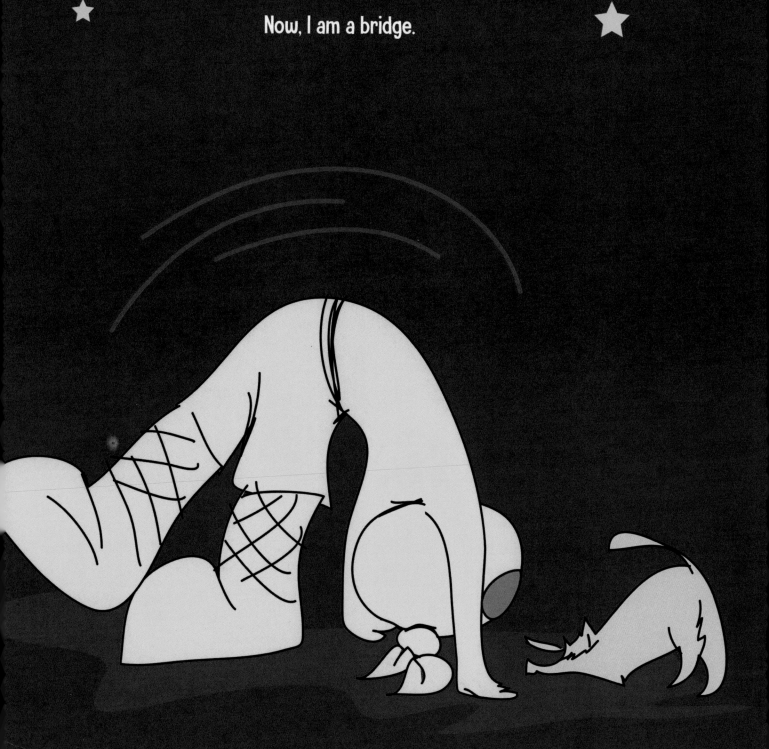

Here's my moon.

My plank helps my back and stomach.

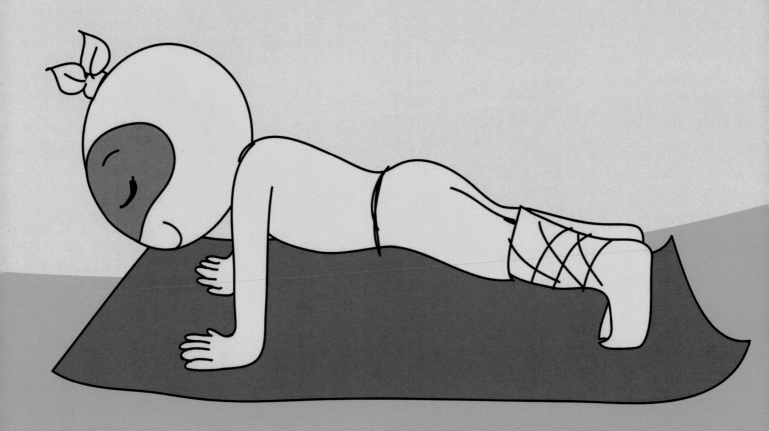

I can get in my child's pose.

The next day, Calm Ninja had several things to do,
and he began to panic.

Suddenly, he remembered something...

He decided to practice the yoga and breathing exercises he learned.

And do you know what happened?

That's right! Calm Ninja remained calm the entire day and every day, thereafter.

He was soon known as the calmest ninja of all.

Your calm mind is the ultimate weapon against life's challenges.

Get our Ninja Life Hacks Journal on Amazon to practice your mindfulness today. And visit NinjaLifeHacks.tv for free printables.

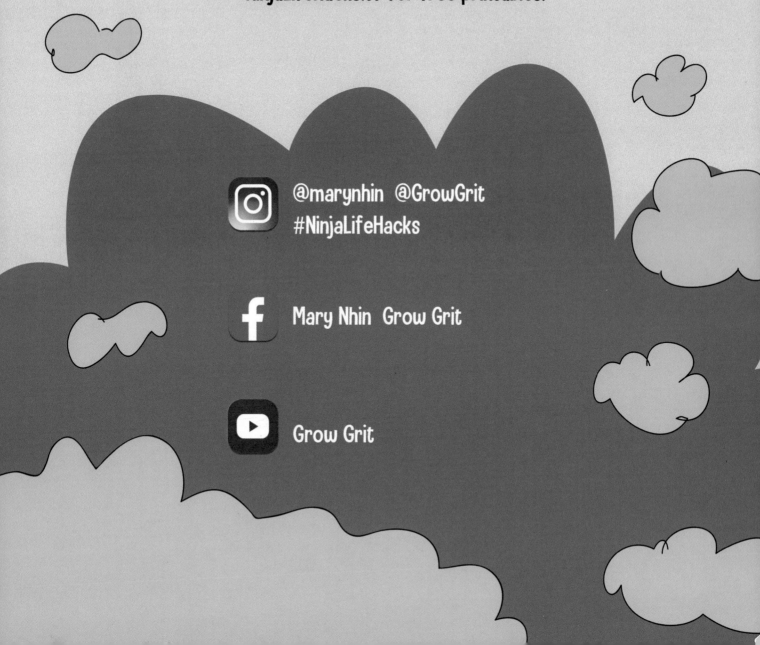

@marynhin @GrowGrit
#NinjaLifeHacks

Mary Nhin Grow Grit

Grow Grit

Made in the USA
Monee, IL
08 January 2021